沙漠

Sharing the Planet | Non-Fiction Series

Copyright © 2022 by Level Learning, INC. and Washington Yu Ying PCS™
Original and Edited Text Copyright © 2022 by Washington Yu Ying PCS™

All rights reserved. No part of this book in whole or part may be reproduced without written permission from the publisher.

Published by Level Learning, INC.
Content Contributors:
Washington Yu Ying PCS™ - Qianyi (Shirley) Zhang, Pearl Zao He You
Level Learning - Jingyao Qi

Illustrations by: Josh Taira

Leveling classification based on Level Learning standard.
For full description, visit www.levellearning.com

ISBN 978-1-64040-056-6
Simplified Chinese Edition

About Level Learning:
Level Learning provides a literacy focused curriculum specifically designed for K-12 Chinese as a Second Language classrooms. Our program offers 20 levels of specific and detailed objectives, leveled texts and passages, mastery-based online assessment, and analytics to enable data-driven instruction. Level Learning reading curriculum for both literature and informational text emphasize grammar and comprehension skills to help teachers develop confident and independent Chinese language readers. The non-fiction series of books are specifically designed to support our informational text course based on multiple national standards. To learn more about our entire offering, visit www.levellearning.com.

About Washington Yu Ying PCS™:
Washington Yu Ying PCS is a Mandarin English dual language immersion International Baccalaureate (IB) World school. Yu Ying's mission is to inspire and prepare young people to create a better world by challenging them to reach their full potential in a nurturing Chinese/English educational environment. Yu Ying's comprehensive IB, dual immersion curriculum equips students with global competencies for success in the real world. As a leader in immersion education, Yu Ying is determined to advance Chinese language programs and global citizenry education by helping other schools create and strengthen their Chinese programs. For more information, email: products@washingtonyuying.org

什么是沙漠？科学家说，每年降雨量不到二百五十四毫米的地方就是沙漠。

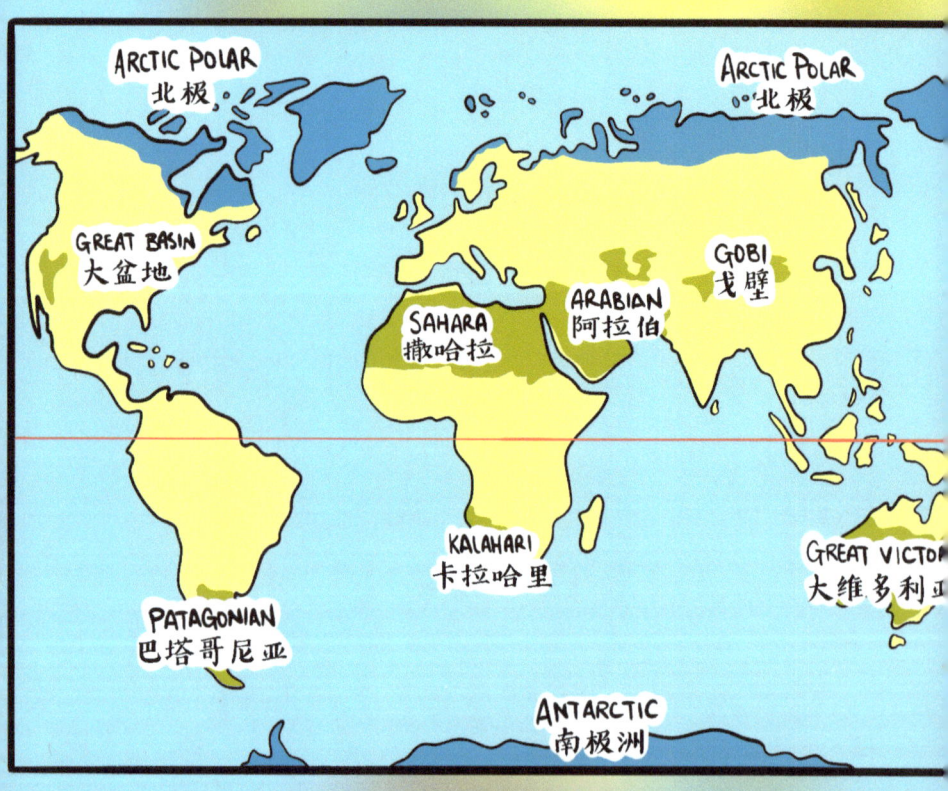

你知道吗？地球上三分之一的陆地都是沙漠。地球上的每个大洲都有沙漠。

有的沙漠气候又干又热，比如非洲撒哈拉大沙漠。撒哈拉大沙漠是世界上最大的热带沙漠。

但是,有的沙漠气候又干又冷,比如在南极洲的沙漠。

在热带沙漠，白天和晚上的温度变化很大。为了能在沙漠生存，这里的动植物都有一些特殊的本领。

骆驼是沙漠里常见的动物。骆驼的驼峰可以储存脂肪和水。骆驼的鼻孔可以闭起来,另外还有长长的睫毛,这些可以帮助骆驼阻挡风沙。

这些特殊的本领可以让骆驼一连几天不吃不喝，在沙漠里穿行。

仙人掌是沙漠里最常见的植物。仙人掌上长满了长长短短的刺。这些刺可以保护仙人掌，还可以帮忙收集空气中的水。仙人掌胖胖的身体可以储存很多水。你知道吗？有的巨人柱仙人掌，可以储存900升水呢！

17

沙漠里的动植物是不是很有趣？你还知道哪些沙漠里的动植物，说说看吧！

Glossary

	Pinyin	English Definition
沙漠	shā mò	desert
科学家	kē xué jiā	scientist
降雨量	jiàng yǔ liàng	rainfall
毫米	háo mǐ	millimeter
三分之一	sān fēn zhī yī	one third
陆地	lù dì	land
大洲	dà zhōu	continent
气候	qì hòu	climate
非洲	fēi zhōu	Africa
撒哈拉大沙漠	sā hā lā dà shā mò	Sahara Desert
热带	rè dài	tropical
南极洲	nán jí zhōu	Antarctica
温度	wēn dù	temperature
变化	biàn huà	change, vary
生存	shēng cún	to survive

	Pinyin	English Definition
特殊	tè shū	special
本领	běn lǐng	ability, skill
骆驼	luò tuo	camel
常见	cháng jiàn	common
驼峰	tuó fēng	camel hump
储存	chǔ cún	to store
脂肪	zhī fáng	fat
鼻孔	bí kǒng	nostril
闭	bì	to close
睫毛	jié máo	eyelashes
阻挡	zǔ dǎng	to block
风沙	fēng shā	sand blown by wind
穿行	chuān xíng	to go through
仙人掌	xiān rén zhǎng	cactus
刺	cì	thorn

Glossary

	Pinyin	English Definition
保护	bǎo hù	to protect
收集	shōu jí	to collect
巨人柱	jù rén zhù	Saguaro cactus (a type of cactus)
升	shēng	liter
有趣	yǒu qù	interesting

www.ingramcontent.com/pod-product-compliance
Lightning Source LLC
Chambersburg PA
CBHW041221070526
44584CB00001B/43